D1477097

MISALLIANCE

Edward Abelson
Illustrated by David Smith

Macdonald

*The author would like to thank Chris Lewis and Tony
Allom at Atlantic Data Systems Ltd.*

A Macdonald Book

Text copyright © Edward Abelson 1989
Illustrations copyright © David Smith 1989

First published in Great Britain in 1989 by
Macdonald & Co (Publishers) Ltd
London & Sydney

British Library Cataloguing in Publication Data
Abelson, Edward
Misalliance.
1. Literature. Writers. Sex relations, to 1980
I. Title   II. Smith, David
306.7 0888

ISBN 0-356-17840-4

Reproduced, printed and bound in Great Britain by
BPCC Hazell Books Ltd
Member of BPCC Ltd
Aylesbury, Bucks, England

Macdonald & Co (Publishers) Ltd
1 New Fetter Lane
London
EC4A 1AR

A Member of Maxwell Pergamon Publishing Corporation plc

CONTENTS

INTRODUCTION

If there is any link between famous writers, apart, of course, from their ability to write, it seems to be that many had disastrous marriages and lovelives. It may be that their failure rate is no greater than average — their fame just makes it more obvious. There is no doubt that there were some extremely unsuitable matches, and that the solitary and single-minded occupation of writing does often make its practitioners rather difficult people to live with. So saying, the best quotations, the best anecdotes and some of the most interesting stories are frequently associated with the lovelives of the literary, and these are the reason — or the excuse — for the compilation of this collection of mis-alliances.

W.H. AUDEN

1907–1973

Auden married a Mann: Erika Mann, daughter of German novelist Thomas. Auden was, in fact, Erika's second choice, suggested by Christopher Isherwood who had turned her down because he was worried that his friends might think he was developing heterosexual tendencies. Auden had no such inhibitions, as he was keen to help Erika Mann obtain British citizenship and escape Nazi Germany. The unlikely union, arranged in the coldest of cold blood, proved oddly satisfactory to both. For Auden there was undoubtedly a certain kudos in being Thomas Mann's son-in-law, and for Erika the marriage put her beyond the clutches of Goebbels, who revoked her German citizenship on the day of the wedding. Auden was soon encouraging all his single male friends to indulge in similar acts of chivalry. Married near Malvern in Worcestershire, they separated immediately, met sporadically over the years, remained firm friends, but never divorced. No hint of passion upset the marriage, which ended with the death of Erika who left Auden a small bequest in gratitude for what he had done. When at some later date Auden was required to fill in his marital status on a form, he wrote 'Widower'.

HONORÉ DE BALZAC
1799–1850

There may have been more unlikely great lovers than Balzac, but not many. It was his immense vitality and charm that enabled him to overcome his natural disadvantages with the opposite sex: his shortness, his obesity, his dress sense — he favoured yellow gloves — and his manners, which owed more to the peasant than the Parisian side of his family. He had a succession of wealthy, aristocratic mistresses, usually much older than himself, of whom the first was Mme de Berny, who was twice his age. Perhaps it was the way that he would chase her around her apartment on all fours that particularly endeared him to her. Anyway, she supported Balzac for seven years until the first volume of what was to become *La Comédie humaine* was published in 1829 and his success as a novelist was assured. During the next 20 years Balzac produced more than 90 books and as his fame spread, he attracted numerous fan letters. One in particular intrigued him: it was postmarked Odessa and signed 'L'Etrangère', and it led him to the great love of his life, Evelina Hanska, a Polish countess. They corresponded and arranged to meet, whereupon, after she had overcome her initial horror at discovering that Balzac looked more like the local butcher than a famous man of letters, they became lovers. Evelina promised that she would marry Balzac when her husband, already old and frail, died; the old count's constitution was more hardy than imagined, however, and he survived another eight years. Obviously not one to be rushed into a second marriage, Evelina kept Balzac waiting for a further 10 years and only relented to his constant proposals just in time. Within six months he was dead, worn out by chasing her halfway across Europe and keeping up his prodigious literary output.

KAREN BLIXEN

1885–1962

As a wedding present to Karen Dinesen and Baron Bror Blixen, Karen's family bought them a coffee plantation in Kenya. His wedding present to her was syphilis. Karen had first fallen in love with Bror's twin brother, Hans, but he had rejected her advances. The twins were her second cousins and as the families continued to meet, Hans's rejection of Karen seemed to increase Bror's interest in her. He kept trying to replace his brother in her affections and eventually his third proposal of marriage was accepted. The prospect of a new start away from Denmark to escape an oppressive home life was an added attraction for Karen. Bror went first to organise everything and on the day she arrived in Mombasa they married. The syphilis was soon evident and soon diagnosed, but the treatment of mercury pills only alleviated the symptoms and never cured her. For the rest of her life she suffered from severe pain in her spine, had lengthy stays in hospital and various operations. Bror proved hopeless both as a husband and as manager of the plantation, carrying on numerous affairs and allowing the coffee business to drift into financial trouble. Karen's only source of happiness was her meeting and subsequent affair with Denys Finch Hatton, an aristocratic English white hunter. Finally Karen and Bror divorced, her family sacked him and she and her brother Thomas tried to salvage something from the mess, but the business had gone too far downhill. The final disaster was when Finch Hatton was killed in a plane crash while on safari. Broken in mind and body, Karen returned to Denmark, where she sought her salvation in writing. *Out of Africa* and *Seven Gothic Tales*, the latter written under the name Isak Dinesen, brought renown and money, but the ravages of syphilis had taken their toll and although she said she lived on oysters and champagne, it was amphetamines that kept her going.

GEORGE GORDON, LORD BYRON

1788–1824

'I have no desire to be better acquainted with Miss Milbank; she is too good for a fallen spirit to know, and I should like her more if she were less perfect.'

Byron was rather premature in his judgement of Miss Annabella Milbanke (and he spelt her name wrong). He was right in that the perfect, priggish Annabella was not the woman for him, but wrong in that he did become better acquainted with her and married her with disastrous results. When the publication of *Childe Harold* made Byron famous, he suddenly found himself much in demand, both sexually and socially, in Regency England. Never one to say no to the ladies or occasionally the boys — he kept a 'seraglio' of maids at Newstead Abbey — Byron's most notorious affair was with Lady Caroline Lamb. Tiring of Caroline, who had scandalised the whole of London with her behaviour in pursuit of him, Byron retreated to the countryside and the charms of Lady Oxford. All the while there were his 'strangely fraternal' feelings for his half-sister Augusta Leigh, with whom he spent more and more time. It was said that Augusta's daughter, Medora, was Byron's, perhaps confirmed by the fact that she and her mother were the beneficiaries of his will, not his wife Annabella and daughter Ada. His marriage to Annabella had all the hallmarks of an arranged match, her money for his title, and Byron was so reluctant that he was a week late for the wedding. His friend Hobhouse wrote: 'Never was a lover less in haste and bridegroom more and more less impatient.' That Byron treated Annabella badly is not in dispute (he took her, for example, for a long stay with Augusta), but their temperaments were so wildly unsuited that no relationship could have lasted. Their daughter Ada was born a year later and within a month they had separated, with Byron being driven into exile by 'the British public in one of its periodical fits of morality'. He resumed his former philandering abroad, first with Mary Shelley's step-sister, Claire Clairmont, and then with various Italian ladies, including Margarita Cogni, 'La Fornarina', and Teresa Guiccioli, whose health acted like a barometer to Byron's presence or absence, much to her husband's annoyance. Shelley's drowning marked the end of the Italian idyll and soon after, Byron's misconceived Greek adventure ended with his death at Missolonghi.

THOMAS CARLYLE

1795–1881

'My dear, whatever you do, never marry a man of genius.'

So wrote Jane Carlyle to a friend, obviously from bitter experience. For a marriage of true minds, made in heaven, ended in hell for both Thomas and Jane. When they first met, she spurned Carlyle's proposals of marriage and kept saying 'no' for five years. As it turned out, these initial impressions were right, but unfortunately she eventually succumbed. She had as formidable an intellect as her

husband, and she was renowned for her conversation, her letter writing and her acid tongue, which was employed mainly against Thomas. To have both at a dinner party was a guarantee of non-stop talk from each in turn, to the exclusion of all other guests. Their host at one party remarked, 'As soon as that man's tongue stops, that woman's begins!' Tennyson said of their relationship (or it may have been Samuel Butler — the same anecdote is ascribed to both) that it was fortunate that the Carlyles married one another as, instead of four people being unhappy, only two were. Butler put the pairing down to God who, he therefore thought, must have a sense of humour. Both had an infinite capacity for making pain for each other and their relationship tended to improve when they were apart, a fairly common occurrence in many marriages. In later life Jane's groundless jealousy of Thomas seemed to precipitate her decline into infirmity and death, after which Thomas so missed the marital conflict that he was unable to produce another book.

CATULLUS

c. 84–c. 54 BC

'Odi et amo. Quare id faciam, fortasse requiris.
Nescio, sed fieri sentio et excrucior.'

These are the lines that Catullus used to sum up his stormy relationship with one of the most notorious Roman women of his day, Clodia Metelli. Enshrined as 'Lesbia' in his poems, Clodia, although of a patrician family, behaved as a high-class courtesan, pursuing Roman low-life with reckless abandon as well as reputedly carrying

on an incestuous affair with her brother and poisoning her husband. Despite her behaviour, or more probably because of it, Catullus was besotted, and his ambivalent attitude towards her is reflected in his poetry with its mixture of tender love poems and vitriolic outpourings cataloguing Clodia's exploits on the street corners of Rome. But it was left to Cicero, the leading Roman advocate, to destroy Clodia in a sensational trial, when he defended another of her lovers, Caelius Rufus, against the charge of trying to poison her. Perhaps she thought her position inviolate as a member of the Roman aristocracy, but nothing could save her from Cicero's demolition job. He gave one of his greatest speeches, holding Clodia up to such ridicule that Caelius' acquittal was a mere formality. His description of her as a 'cheap Clytemnestra' with her statue of Venus adorned with mementos of all her lovers left little to the imagination and Clodia's life in ruins. The allusions were not lost on the crowded courtroom, where perhaps Catullus was an interested spectator; he was so pleased with the result that he composed a little 'Thank You' ode to the Prince of Lawyers. Clodia and her brother were disgraced and their names ceased to be mentioned, but Catullus' triumph was short-lived, for within two years he was dead.

GEOFFREY CHAUCER

c. 1340–1400

> 'Lo, *whiche sleightes and subtilities*
> *In wommen been! for ay as bisy as bees*
> *Ben they, us sely men for to deceyve,*
> *And from a sothe ever wol they weyve.'*

Chaucer may have been the Father of English poetry, but was he the father of his children? His own father held a position on the periphery of court life, where Chaucer himself might have expected to remain, had he not come under the protection and patronage of John of Gaunt. John was King Edward III's son, and after the death of his elder brother, the Black Prince, he became the richest and most powerful nobleman in England. Chaucer owed his advancement to a position as a top civil servant and eventually to Member of Parliament entirely to John of Gaunt's influence, or maybe his wife's. Chaucer was to become John of Gaunt's quasi brother-in-law, because he married Philippa de Roet, sister of Katherine Swynford, John's long-time mistress. Fourteenth-century gossip has it that Philippa too was John's mistress — perhaps he liked to keep it in the family — and that Chaucer's acquiescence in this state of affairs accounted for his preferment and maybe also for his numerous diplomatic trips abroad. The marriage does not seem to have been a great success, with Chaucer writing about the 'sorwe and wo that is in mariage', and he was also accused by one Cecilia Chaumpaigne of rape, '*violentus concubitus*', not something that a man with a happy home life normally indulges in. Philippa had died before her sister became John of Gaunt's third wife, but Chaucer's position was already assured when John's son, Henry IV, came to the throne. He died in the second year of Henry's reign and was buried in a corner of Westminster Abbey, not on account of his poetry, but for his services to the Crown, though it was in fact this part of the Abbey that eventually became Poet's Corner.

AGATHA CHRISTIE

1890–1976

The mystery of Agatha Christie's ten-day disappearance in 1926 has never been satisfactorily explained. When a famous crime writer and novelist leaves home unexpectedly and her car is found abandoned not far away the next day, it creates a sensation. Was it suicide, murder, amnesia or a hoax? All these theories featured in the headline news, but the press and the police were mystified. Her husband, the war hero Colonel Archibald Christie, was away on the day of her disappearance, and slowly various pieces of the puzzle revealed themselves. Agatha had been desperately unhappy. The Christies had just moved into a new house which she hated and which had a reputation for bringing bad luck to its occupants; her mother, to whom she had been devoted, had just died; and Archie had announced that he had fallen in love with a fellow golfer, Nancy Neele, and was spending most of his time in London. It was a member of Mr Harry Codd's band, the resident orchestra at the Hydropathic Hotel, Harrogate, who first recognised Agatha, and she and Archie were reunited. She seemed to have lost her memory and had even advertised in *The Times* asking for information about 'Theresa Neele', the name under which she was registered at the hotel. Her discovery posed more questions that it answered, and speculation continued unabated. Was it a *cri de coeur*, was it a publicity stunt, was it done to embarrass Archie, who might even have been charged with her murder if she had remained undiscovered, or was it to work out a plot for a new story? No one really knew the answer and her explanation of memory loss was grudgingly accepted. It does seem suitably appropriate for such a woman to devise a mystery to which she alone knew the solution. She and Archie were divorced, he went off and married his Nancy and she had a very happy second marriage with the renowned archaeologist Max Mallowan. It is ironic that she is best known by the name she carried for the shortest period of her life, linked for ever to a man she came to hate.

SAMUEL TAYLOR COLERIDGE

1772–1834

'If any woman wanted an exact and copious Recipe, "How to make a Husband compleatly miserable", I could furnish her with one.'

Coleridge's thoughts on marriage were a calumny on his wife. Had it not been for a friend arranging a partner for Coleridge, it is doubtful whether he would have ever married at all. He was a hopeless case, an unworldly dreamer who had no conception of obligations and duties, particularly those of a husband. Not surprisingly his one excursion into married life was an unmitigated disaster. The unfortunate woman was one of three Fricker sisters whom the poet Robert Southey chose as suitable brides for himself, Coleridge and another friend, Robert Lovell. The idea was for the three couples to set up a Utopian community in America, but they got no further than Bristol. The only part of the plan that came to fruition was the arranged marriages, with Southey taking Edith Fricker and allotting Sara to Coleridge and Mary to Lovell. Coleridge had to be cajoled by Southey into going through with the arrangement and was led protesting to the altar. The opium habit that Coleridge started just after his marriage may have resulted in '*Kubla Khan*', but it also made him even more vague and unreliable than before. He spent sufficient time with Sara to produce several children, but not much longer. It fell to Southey to support his sister-in-law, a task that he found not too unbearable as he realised that he had chosen wrongly and much preferred Sara. Coleridge, in the meantime, had fallen in love with Sarah Hutchinson, sister of Wordsworth's wife Mary, but his love went unreciprocated. As the opium gained stronger hold, Coleridge became more reliant on the generosity of various friends and spent the last 18 years of his life in the care of a doctor in Highgate, London, where finally he found an equilibrium of sorts.

COLETTE
1873–1954

When she married, Sidonie-Gabrielle Colette was a naïve provincial girl, and her betrothal to the sophisticated Parisian journalist Henri Gauthier-Villars may have been part of a business arrangement between their fathers, who were old friends. Henri, 15 years older than Colette and better known under his *nom de plume* of Willy, ran a literary factory in Paris where various hacks churned out books, articles and reviews which he appropriated and which all appeared under his name. One day he suggested to Colette that she might have some reminiscences about her schooldays, and the result was *Claudine à l'école* which was published under Willy's name. The book was an immediate and immense success, and a series of equally successful Claudine sequels followed. If you think that spin-offs from best-sellers are new phenomena, then think again. Paris was inundated with Claudine-related products, amongst them Claudine perfume, Claudine ice-cream and even Claudine cigarettes. Unfortunately Colette got none of the credit for the books and very little of the vast amounts of money that started to roll in, though for the first time in their marriage Willy very generously gave her an allowance. The relationship had always seemed loveless and now, with Colette becoming just another one of Willy's authors, it became the business arrangement it always appeared. If she had any doubts, they were dispelled early on when she discovered Willy with one of his mistresses. Living in the Parisian demi-monde Colette had soon lost her naïvety, become a lesbian and discovered a passion and a limited talent for acting; when she and Willy inevitably parted, she went on the music-hall stage, where she appeared with her new lover, the Marquise de Belboeuf, nicknamed 'Missy'. It was in the middle of this affair that she went off with Auguste Hériot, the model for Chéri in her famous book of the same name. This is the story of the relationship between a young man and an older woman, and Colette herself was the model for Léa, the female character. Although Missy approved of the partnership and although Auguste was heir to a vast fortune, she never loved him and instead married Henri de Jouvenel, the editor of *Le Matin*, a Paris newspaper. It was her third marriage, to Maurice Goudeket, that was the first to bring her true happiness, an elusive state that perhaps she only found before with Missy.

DANTE ALIGHIERI

1265–1321

'Ella non parea figliuola d'uomo mortale, ma di deo.'

Dante tells us that he met and fell in love with his
Beatrice when he was only nine and she eight, not so
unusual in an age when children were betrothed at birth or
even earlier. He also writes that he fainted, aged one, at the
moment of her birth, a story that does seem rather unlikely.
Beatrice was a Portinari, a member of a wealthy Florentine
banking family, whereas Dante was an Alighieri, a mere
moneylender from a lower social stratum, and therefore
marriage between the two was unthinkable. When he was
12, Dante was betrothed to Gemma Donati, and at about
the same time the Portinari betrothed Beatrice to Simone di
Bardi. When Simone and Beatrice did wed, the marriage
was very short-lived as she died aged only 24. Dante,
himself not yet married, was heartbroken and his family
made him marry Gemma to console him. It didn't work. He
had already celebrated Beatrice and his love for her in his
poetry, and from then on until his death more than 30 years
later she became his obsession, a most upsetting experience
for Mrs Gemma Alighieri. That may explain why, when
Dante was exiled from Florence for his political activities,
Gemma chose not to accompany him and why, when an
amnesty was announced, Dante chose not to return. Instead
he spent the last 20 years of his life alone wandering around
the map of Italy. Just before he died, Dante completed his
masterpiece *The Divine Comedy*, in which, after being
guided through the nether regions by the poet Virgil, it is
Beatrice who is his guide to Paradise.

CHARLES DICKENS

1812–1870

Dickens made the same mistake as Robert Southey: he married the wrong sister. His first love was Maria Beadnell, the daughter of a banker who thought Dickens, the son of a mere and bankrupt clerk, an unworthy match. Maria was sent to Paris to forget, which she did, but Dickens never did. Instead he married Catherine Hogarth, whose younger sister, Mary, came to live with them soon after the marriage. The tragic death of Mary a year later profoundly affected Dickens; he was unable to work, with an instalment of *Oliver Twist* being postponed for a month

and the image of Mary haunting his dreams. Dickens used both Maria and Mary, but never his wife, Catherine, as models for those perfect heroines that always seem to inhabit his novels. Mary was soon replaced by yet another Hogarth sister, Georgina, who bore a striking resemblance to her and acted as a continual reminder of Mary to Dickens. Georgina became indispensable in the running of the Dickens' household to the extent that when Charles and Catherine eventually separated, Georgina stayed. The reason for the separation was Dickens' infatuation and love affair with a young actress, Ellen Ternan, but she never moved into Gadshill, where the mistress of the house continued to be Georgina. And it was the faithful Georgina who ministered to Dickens on his death-bed.

JOHN DONNE
1572–1631

'*No, no. The falt was mine, impute it to me,*
Or rather to conspiring destinie,
Which (since I lov'd for forme before) decreed,
That I should suffer when I lov'd indeed.'

'The Remarkable Error of His Life' was how Isaak Walton described Donne's marriage. A promising political career was ruined when John Donne met and fell in love with Anne More. In order to advance himself, Donne, who came from a Catholic family — his younger brother, Henry, was gaoled in Newgate for hiding a priest and died there — had to convert to Protestantism before he became private secretary to Sir Thomas Egerton, Lord Keeper of the Great Seal. It was in this position that Donne first met the 14-year-old Anne More, a niece of Sir Thomas's wife. When Anne was 18 they married secretly without either the consent of her father, who was so furious that he had Donne thrown into prison and his daughter returned home, or the consent of his patron, who dismissed him. After obtaining his release Donne had to go through the courts to get his wife back. Her father relented and John and Anne were reunited, though without the benefit of her dowry, but Egerton did not and Donne was deprived of his livelihood. With his secular advancement curtailed Donne suffered 15 years of hardship and poverty, living on the charity of his wife's relations until he took Holy Orders. There then followed a spectacular rise through the church hierarchy, culminating in his appointment as Dean of St Paul's and his role as friend and spiritual adviser to both James I and Charles I. Donne reputedly composed the following verse on his marriage to Anne More and its consequences:

'John Donne,
Anne Donne,
Un-done.'

JOHN DRYDEN
1631–1700

'Here lies my wife: here let her lie!
Now she's at rest, and so am I.'

Unfortunately Dryden's intended epitaph for his wife was never used as she survived him, albeit going mad soon after his death. The verse's implication was true: Dryden and his wife never did get on. He was bullied into marrying Lady Elizabeth Howard by her brother Sir Robert, with whom he had collaborated on the play *The Indian Queen*. This method of arranging a marriage rarely leads to a satisfactory relationship and so it proved in this case. Neither Dryden's nor Lady Elizabeth's reputation was completely unsullied before their marriage and by persuading Dryden to take his sister off his hands, Sir Robert was able to uphold the honour of the Howards. Throughout his life Dryden bent with the prevailing wind, a eulogy to Cromwell followed a year later by one on the Restoration, conversion to Catholicism on the accession of James II and this forced marriage into aristocracy. He soon found, however, that he was treated as a social inferior by his wife and her friends, and he sought comfort and consolation at the theatre in the company of his mistress, an actress. Perhaps this was the reason that he became such a prolific playwright, an occupation that, on the whole, he found very distasteful. Amongst his vast output was *Paradise Lost*, the musical, created with the approval of Milton himself! When not at the theatre or at Will's Coffee House in Covent Garden, Dryden was always to be found in his study where one day he was upbraided by the neglected Lady Elizabeth: 'Lord, Mr Dryden, how can you always be poring over those musty books? I wish I were a book and then I should have more of your company.' 'Pray my dear' replied Dryden 'if you do become a book let it be an almanack, for then I shall change you every year.'

T.S. ELIOT

1888–1965

> '*Will T.S. Eliot please return to his home 68 Clarence Gate Gardens which he abandoned Sept. 17th 1932. Keys with WLJ*'

This plaintive advertisement was placed in the Personal columns of *The Times* by Eliot's wife, Vivien, on the second anniversary of his desertion. In 1932 he had sailed to

America to lecture at Harvard for a year, knowing that this enforced separation would enable him to make the break with his wife by default. The next time they met after his return was in a solicitor's office where he was unable to look her in the eye. Unwilling to accept the inevitable, and desperate for a reconciliation, she relentlessly pursued Eliot at work, at the theatre and in the press. The signs of her mental instability had always been there and from the very start their marriage had been a nightmare, exacerbated by her brief infidelity with Bertrand Russell, her constant ill-health, and Eliot's indifference. Vivien's family eventually had her committed to an asylum where she spent the rest of her life. She and Eliot never divorced. Eliot's callousness and cruelty to those closest to him was again evident when he eventually remarried. Without a word to his companion of 10 years, the crippled John Hayward, or to the two women, Emily Hale and Mary Trevelyan, who had befriended him after the break-up of his marriage, he left his flat very early one January morning to marry his secretary from Faber and Faber at 6.15 a.m. so as not to disrupt the routine of his life. About the lives of John, Mary and Emily he was not quite so considerate, or perhaps from the man with the 'twinkling personality' whose idea of fun was to go to the BBC in a false moustache, it was just another joke.

EDWARD FITZGERALD

1809–1883

'*Marriage is standing at your desk all ready for your work with your brain clear and then seeing the door open and a great big bonnet asking you to go for a walk with it.*'

'A very doubtful experiment' was what Fitzgerald predicted for his marriage, and he was right. He led a very contented bachelor existence amongst the Victorian literati in thrall to his flamboyant mother's personality and

money. It was only a rash promise to a dying friend, Bernard Barton, to look after his daughter that led Fitzgerald to the altar. Even then he was in no great rush to fulfil his promise, and it was only after a seven-year engagement and after the death of his mother that he married Lucy Barton. She was fat and 48 and Fitzgerald was 47. He set the tone by refusing to dress up for the wedding, attending in his oldest and sloppiest clothes, with Lucy, in contrast, appearing like mutton dressed up as Little Bo Peep. The marriage lasted four months. Lucy was pensioned off and retired to Croydon, where she became so gross that she was unable even to get out of her armchair. Fitzgerald returned to his former way of life and to completing his *Rubaiyat of Omar Khayyam*. When first published, *The Rubaiyat* was ignored and it was only after Rossetti rescued a copy from a remainder bin and spread the word that its popularity was assured. With Fitzgerald's name missing from the frontispiece of this and subsequent editions, no one except close friends knew of his involvement. Utterly unaffected by fame, Fitzgerald spent the last years of his life cruising the North Sea in his yacht and in the company of an Aldeburgh fisherman, 'Posh' Fletcher.

F. SCOTT FITZGERALD

1896–1940

'There are no second acts in American lives.'

The perpetrator of the myth of the Jazz Age was destroyed by his own creation. The success that his books brought Scott Fitzgerald enabled him and his wife

Zelda to live up to their own images. Whereas he just about survived the twenties as an alcoholic wreck in debt, Zelda, always teetering on the brink of insanity, did not, and their perfect marriage was destroyed. Fitzgerald had returned from the First World War to reclaim and marry his Southern belle, Zelda Sayre. Initially the writing paid for the constant partying and the drinking, the high life in Paris and on the Côte d'Azur, but the fast and riotous living in which each egged the other on to more outrageous excesses eventually took its toll and it became more difficult to write to replenish their pocket books. By the end of the decade tastes had changed, Fitzgerald was no longer in fashion, and the tone of his books had changed, too, from the optimism of *This Side of Paradise* to the physical and emotional detritus in *Tender is the Night*, where the schizophrenic Nicole Diver is a thinly disguised portrait of Zelda. Her schizophrenia led to her being institutionalised first in France, then back in America. There were the occasional remissions that promised a full recovery for Zelda, but it never materialised. By now Scott was tubercular as well as an alcoholic, and in an attempt to pick up the pieces of his writing career he headed west to Hollywood. A relationship with gossip columnist Sheilah Graham finally brought him a little stability and happiness, but it didn't last. He was only 44 when a heart attack killed him. Zelda survived him for seven years when, about to be released from her mental hospital, she was burnt to death in a fire.

GUSTAVE FLAUBERT

1821–1880

'Madame Bovary, c'est moi.'

The first time Flaubert fell in love was a holiday romance in Trouville: he was 15 and the object of his affection was a married lady of 26, Elisa Schlesinger. They met later in Paris where Flaubert blurted out his true feelings for Elisa, who, though flattered, gently told him that she was not prepared to have an affair with him. Then fate, in the shape of an epileptic fit, determined for Flaubert that he would never marry. After his first attack at the age of 23, he gave up his chosen career in the law and devoted himself to a life of literature. For someone who had confessed that he detested humanity, this was probably a great relief as he was able to live a very sheltered provincial life in Normandy with his mother. If in any way Flaubert modelled Emma Bovary on himself, it was as a provincial with dreams of a world outside and the inability to share in it. Even on his trips to Paris he managed to have a quiet time, mostly with his mistress Louise Colet, a poet and novelist. He told friends that every time he made love to Louise, he was thinking of Elisa. The worst news for any Frenchman is to hear of the death of his mistress's husband and so it proved for Flaubert. When Louise's husband died, she appeared on Flaubert's doorstep in the country demanding that he marry her. He treated her appallingly, physically threw her out and they never met again. Finally, 35 years after he first fell in love with Elisa, Flaubert heard that her husband had died. They corresponded, they met, but he was no longer 15 nor she 26 and they parted. So he only ever made love to Elisa in his imagination.

FORD MADOX FORD

1873–1939

Ford Madox Ford had four wives, three marriages and there were two Mrs Madox Fords, an apparent and strange anomaly, mainly brought about by his several changes of name. He was born Ford Hermann Hueffer, the son of the German-born music critic of *The Times* and the grandson of the Pre-Raphaelite painter Ford Madox Brown. To please his grandfather, who brought him up after the early death of his father, and various continental relations, he first changed his name to Joseph Leopold Ford Hermann Madox Hueffer, eventually shortened to Ford Madox Hueffer, under which name he married his first wife, Elsie Martindale. Since her father disapproved because of Ford's Bohemian background and Elsie's age — she was only 17 — they eloped. For 10 years they lived in the country, where he struggled to earn a living as a writer, before he left for London to further his literary career. Here he came under the spell of Violet Hunt, who, with her mother, ran a literary and artistic salon for the great and good of Edwardian London. Ford, though 17 years younger, wanted to marry Violet and asked Elsie for a divorce. She refused and sued him for 'Restitution of Conjugal Rights'. Ford and Violet fled to Germany, where, because of his father, he thought that he could qualify for German nationality and be divorced there. However, duped by a lawyer, he was unsuccessful, but it was reported in an English paper that he had married Violet. Elsie was so incensed that she sued for libel and won. The case left Ford penniless, and for a while he wrote under the name of Daniel Chaucer to avoid his creditors. It didn't prevent Violet from calling herself Mrs Hueffer nor Elsie from continuous litigation. When he ran off with an Australian painter, Stella Bowen, he changed his name to Ford Madox Ford to avoid there being three Mrs Hueffers. His affair with Jean Rhys broke up that relationship, after which a genuine second marriage to Janice Biala was to see out his last years.

GEORGE GISSING

1857–1903

'*Marriage rarely means happiness, either for man or woman.*'

For Gissing it certainly didn't. The unrelieved gloom and melancholy of Gissing's books is just a reflection of his life, living in garrets, struggling against poverty and lack of recognition — the life of a hack-writer. On top of all that he displayed a remarkably poor judgement in his choice of wives. A brilliant academic career was ruined when he was caught stealing money from fellow students at Owen's College, Manchester, money he needed to support and reform his lover Helen Harrison, a Manchester prostitute. Disgraced and sent to prison for a short spell, he then emigrated to America, where for a year he nearly starved trying to earn his living as a journalist. He returned, immediately married Helen and took her off to London. There they lived in various seedy lodging houses, and as the marriage disintegrated, Helen returned to her old profession, whoring and drinking herself into comas, into hospital and finally into the grave. Learning nothing from that experience, Gissing married again, again to an ill-educated working-class girl, Edith Underwoood, whom he met at a music-hall and who neither cared nor understood about his work. Seven years of misery followed, with Gissing being physically assaulted by his wife, until she was carted off to the asylum. Unable to get a divorce, he fled to France where he married, bigamously, Gabrielle Fleury, his French translator. But even then, with a life of comparative comfort and the company of a woman his social and intellectual equal, Gissing, so used to his previous deprivations, was still not content, finding fault with everything French, especially the food. Anyway the complaints didn't last long, as after four years in France he caught pneumonia and died.

THOMAS HARDY

1840–1928

Behind the heavily curtained window of Max Gate, Hardy's self-designed Gothic Dorset home, there existed a strange *ménage à trois*, only Mrs Hardy was an unknowing participant. As a literary celebrity in late Victorian England, Hardy attracted various literary ladies, one of whom, Florence Dugdale, he fell in love with and then managed to insinuate into his household. He engineered a meeting between her and his wife Emma, who, just as Hardy had planned, invited Florence to join them at Max Gate as her companion and his amanuensis. The strange

ménage continued with Emma, a semi-invalid, only joining Thomas and Florence downstairs for dinner each day. The death of Emma had a profound effect on Hardy and his indifference to the live Emma was replaced by a veneration of his dead wife, manifested in a flood of poetry recalling their life together. Hardy, totally oblivious to Emma's pain-wracked final years, sought some form of absolution by making a pilgrimage to all the places that he and Emma had known when they were courting, this time dragging the complaining Florence along. After a decent period of mourning had been observed, Hardy did marry Florence, though at first it was secret as he confessed to a friend 'I was under the strictest orders not to tell anyone.' When news of the marriage eventually broke, Florence was described as 'an old friend of Emma's'. Although Florence had attained the position to which she had always aspired — that of Thomas Hardy's wife — there was a bitterness and a hollowness to the achievement. Hardy's guilt reanimated Emma, who still remained an ever-present barrier between them, and Hardy resented the isolation that the over-protective Florence, with the help of the dog Wessex, brought in her cultivation of his image as the Grand Old Man of English letters. Mistresses, it seems, don't always make good wives, nor lovers good husbands, as both Thomas and Florence discovered, and the marriage was never the idyll that either imagined it might have been.

JAROSLAV HAŠEK
1883–1923

Anarchist, practical-joker, a true Bohemian in both senses of the word, Jaroslav Hašek, author of *The Good Soldier Švejk*, had as much difficulty in sustaining relationships as he had in holding down jobs. His first proper job as editor of a popular animal magazine was his attempt to ingratiate himself with his prospective father-in-law. It worked, and he was allowed to marry Jarmila, but predictably Hašek was soon out of a job. Fed up with writing about fowl pest, he started to invent stories about plagues of muskrats and insert spurious advertisements for 'thoroughbred werewolves'. When his next project, selling mutts as pedigree dogs, ran into trouble with the law, Jarmila went home to mother. Hašek, depressed, was stopped from throwing himself off a Prague bridge into the Vltava by a passing theatrical hairdresser and instead was locked up in an asylum for a while. He was reunited with his wife for the birth of their son, but when the in-laws arrived to wet the baby's head he popped out to get some celebratory beer and never returned. Various careers followed including journalist, cabaret star and leader of his own political party. Called up in the First World War by the Czech army, source of many of Švejk's humourous misadventures, Hašek's career as a soldier lasted only six months before he was captured by the Russians. Harsh Russian treatment soon persuaded him to join the Czech Legion to fight against the Germans. The October Revolution changed all that, and the Legion found itself fighting for the White Russians against the Reds, but without Hašek, who had deserted to become a Commissar in the Red Army. After this unlikely career as a minor Soviet official, he returned to Prague with a new Russian wife. Pursued by Jarmila and the Czech police and prosecuted for bigamy, Hašek abandoned both his wives and fled to the country. Worn out by his dissolute living and by now an enormous 24 stone, he was unable to enjoy the belated success of *Švejk* and died aged only 40.

WILLIAM HAZLITT
1778–1830

'I was at Hazlitt's marriage, and had like to have been turned out several times during the ceremony. Anything awful makes me laugh. I misbehaved once at a funeral.'

This was Charles Lamb reminiscing about Hazlitt's first wedding. The remarks were slightly churlish of him, as it was he and his sister Mary who had introduced their friend Sarah Stoddart to Hazlitt and encouraged them to marry. The realisation that perhaps he had done the wrong thing may account for his behaviour in church. Lamb always was a practical joker. William and Sarah soon led separate lives, he immersed in his painting and writing and she in vast walking tours. In 1820 Hazlitt met and fell passionately in love with Sarah Walker, the daughter of the house where he lodged. He was 43, she 19, and Augustine Birrell said of the affair 'A fool at 40 is a fool indeed.' Hazlitt's extremely frank account of his unrequited infatuation, *Liber Amoris*, appalled his friends and delighted his enemies. These latter now included Coleridge and Wordsworth, his former radical friends, who had joined the forces of reaction, much to Hazlitt's disgust, and who resurrected and embroidered the story of a similar infatuation of Hazlitt's years before in the Lakes. The affair with Sarah W. petered out, the marriage to Sarah S. ended in divorce and Hazlitt married again, this time to a rich widow, Mrs Bridgewater, and again with a conspicuous lack of success. They honeymooned in Italy and France, where the second Mrs Hazlitt remained when he returned to London. When he wrote to inquire politely when she might return, she replied that she had no intention of ever returning. They never met again. Hazlitt's dying words were 'Well, I've had a happy life', but the facts seem to dispute that.

ERNEST HEMINGWAY

1899–1961

As one biographer points out, Hemingway and Byron had one thing in common — they both owned boats! They also had several lovers. Hemingway once confessed to a friend: 'The trouble is, I'm a fool for women; I always have to marry them.' He did — four of them. He always managed to have a prospective new wife ready before he divorced his old one. It might have been five if Gertrude Stein hadn't turned him down, probably at Alice B. Toklas's insistence — now that would have been an odd combination.

VICTOR HUGO

1802–1885

The first casualty of Victor-Marie Hugo's marriage to Adèle Foucher was his brother Eugène, who, prone to madness, went completely insane for he too was in love with Adèle. The second casualty was the marriage itself. For the virginal Victor made up for lost time and made love to Adèle nine times during that first night (or so he said), and he immediately discovered an insatiable appetite for sex which his wife was unable to satisfy. His major mistress for 50 years was the actress Juliette Drouet, who even followed him into exile when his republicanism made remaining in Paris impossible. The exile lasted 20 years, first in Brussels, then in Guernsey where Juliette found a house overlooking Hugo's, greatly to Adèle's annoyance. The only rival to Juliette's pre-eminence as Hugo's main mistress was Léonie Briard, whose husband, fed up with her behaviour, informed the police. An inspector followed Léonie to a small apartment in Paris and broke in to discover her and Hugo *in flagrante delicto*. The apartment was one of several, rented under various pseudonyms, that Hugo kept in and around the city to accommodate his mistresses. Under the *Code Napoléon*, the legal system in France at the time, wives were treated as minors with no rights and subject to their husbands, so poor Léonie was dragged off to prison, while Hugo as a peer of France was above the law. After the overthrow of the monarchy in 1870, Hugo returned to Paris a hero and carried on much as before. Adèle had by now died, and while his affair with Juliette continued, he refused to marry her and found a younger generation of new mistresses, including Sarah Bernhardt and the daughter of his best friend, Théophile Gautier. Edmond Goncourt was in awe of Hugo's sexual athleticism, which continued into his eighties, right up to his death. Goncourt relates that on Hugo's death all the prostitutes in Paris went into mourning, and the night before the funeral was one massive 'priapic orgy' as they gave away their services free to the citizens of Paris *en plein air* on the Champs-Élysées.

EDWARD GEORGE EARLE LYTTON BULWER-LYTTON, LORD LYTTON

1803–1873

'I know a villain, and have one in my eye at this moment that would far eclipse anything that I have read of in books. Don't think that I am drawing on my imagination. The man is alive and constantly under my gaze. In fact he is my own husband.'

This was Lady Lytton writing to Wilkie Collins to say that her husband far eclipsed the villainous Count Fosco in *The Woman in White*. The Lyttons had been separated for more than 20 years when she wrote this and her vendetta never lessened. Theirs was a dark and stormy marriage and after the acrimonious break-up, she continually harrassed her husband through the courts, in print and at his election meetings. It was against his mother's wishes that Edward Bulwer Lytton married Rosina Wheeler, 'a woman of excitable temperament', and mother knew best. She bombarded him with lawsuits, wrote a novel *Cheveley or The Man of Honour* with Edward as the villain, and had to be dragged screaming and protesting from one of his adoption meetings. All this seemed to have little effect on his dual career as a politician and as a writer of turgid novels almost as long as his name. His contemporary Disraeli was more successful at both, though less fecund as a novelist. Rosina was certified insane for a while, but was released to continue her demented pursuit. The broken family home did no apparent harm to their son, who became Viceroy of India and Lytton Strachey's godfather.

KATHERINE MANSFIELD

1888–1923

Appearances can be deceptive. Behind the mask of a frail Japanese doll that Katherine Mansfield affected, there lurked a rampant bisexual All Black. Her first sexual experiences were adolescent lesbian affairs in her native New Zealand, from where she escaped to London at the earliest opportunity. Within a year of her arrival she was pregnant

and married, but the father of the child and the husband were not the same man. When she had discovered that she was pregnant by one of her lovers, she hastily accepted a proposal of marriage from George Bowden, a man she hardly knew and never did get to know as the marriage, unconsummated, lasted less than a day. Katherine deserted him on the morning after to return to Ida Baker, 'her wife', as she called her. Ida had idolised Katherine ever since their meeting at a school for young ladies, and at most times of crisis in her life Ida was at hand to provide help and consolation. Sent to Germany to have the baby, Katherine miscarried, but it was there that she met a Polish writer, Floryan Sobieniewski, who was to have a profound effect on her life. Floryan left her with two legacies, a love of Chekhov stories and gonorrhea; the first provided the inspiration for her writing, the second permanently impaired her health and led to an early death from TB. Her first published short story was a reworking of a Chekhov story, which prompted Floryan to reappear later in Katherine's life to blackmail her successfully for the plagiarism. John Middleton Murry, initially her lodger, then her occasional lover and finally her second husband, never fully understood Katherine, and their relationship was punctuated by long periods apart. Murry had to be summoned to Katherine's deathbed and for once Ida was not there, arriving a day late. The rest of Murry's life was spent as the maker and the keeper of the flame of Katherine's reputation, and having three more attempts at marriage. Wife number two resembled Katherine Mansfield to such an extent she even contracted and died of TB, number three only lasted a short time, but number four was a success.

W. SOMERSET MAUGHAM

1874–1965

Somerset Maugham was an unlikely candidate for marriage as he was, as he put it, 'a quarter normal and three quarters queer.' Early in his life, after an initial homosexual encounter, he tried to persuade himself that it was the other way round, and he had various heterosexual affairs, amongst which was one with Violet Hunt, novelist and literary lion-hunter. This attempt at respectability culmin-

ated in a most unsatisfactory and unhappy marriage to the famous Dr Barnardo's daughter Syrie, who, having previously shown a marked predilection for extremely wealthy expatriate Americans, transferred her attentions to this celebrated wealthy English writer. When they first met she was the wife of Henry Wellcome of the eponymous drug company, and was also the mistress of Gordon Selfridge of the eponymous store. Her affair with Maugham dragged on over several continents and seven years until eventually they married, two years after the birth of their daughter, Liza, Syrie's divorce from Wellcome being long and drawn out. Unfortunately for Syrie, Maugham in the meantime had met the great love of his life, Gerald Haxton, while working for the Red Cross during the First World War. Later on in the war Haxton, an American, while on leave in England, was tried for gross indecency and although acquitted was deported as an undesirable alien on his next attempt to return. This meant that to be with Gerald, Maugham needed to live abroad, which he did for six months every year. The other six months he spent in London with Syrie, trying to keep up some pretence of togetherness, which was difficult as Syrie tended to rent out their London home when he was away to get her own back on him. Their divorce in 1929, although it freed Maugham to live fulltime with Gerald in France, did nothing to lessen the acrimony and bitchiness that filled their marriage. The final act was when he, fearful of being certified as insane by his daughter, tried to disinherit Liza and adopt Gerald's replacement, Alan Searle. Maugham was 86 and Searle 58. His argument was that since Syrie had not been divorced at the time of Liza's birth, he was not legally the father. He lost and remained bitter and resentful of any reminder of Syrie.

GEORGE MEREDITH

1828–1909

*'Like sculptured effigies they might be seen
Upon their marriage-tomb, the sword between;
Each wishing for the sword that severs all.'*

At the Royal Academy exhibition of 1856 one painting created a sensation. It was *The Death of Chatterton* by Henry Wallis, and the model for that famous image of the pallid poet lying on his deathbed was George Meredith. Renowned for his striking good looks and chestnut red hair, Meredith was married to Mary Ellen, the 'flighty' widowed daughter of the satirist and novelist Thomas Love Peacock, who, while disliking his son-in-law's constant smoking, helped to establish his literary career. But while the languid Meredith posed, Mary Ellen fell for Henry Wallis and ran off with him to Capri. Meredith's son described the episode

as: 'Two highly strung temperaments — man and wife — each imaginative, emotional, quick to anger, cuttingly satirical in dispute, each an incomparable wielder of the rapier of ridicule, could not find domestic content within the narrow bounds of poverty and lodgings.' Meredith himself put it rather differently and rather more succinctly: 'The marriage was a blunder.' Mary Ellen's affair with Wallis was soon over once the initial passion had subsided on both sides and she begged Meredith to let her return to him and their son. But he was adamant in his refusal and within a few years she had drunk herself to death. Although he did remarry, the memory of his first attempt and the remorse at his treatment of Mary Ellen remained with him always and was never far from the surface of all that he subsequently wrote. In the poem *Modern Love* Meredith charts the course and the breakdown of his relationship with Mary Ellen. Wallis lived for a further 60 years and never produced another painting of note.

JOHN MILTON

1608–1674

For a man living in seventeenth-century England, Milton came to marriage rather late, preferring a life of study and contemplation. He finally chose as his wife a 17-year-old girl (half his age), Mary Powell, who, on being brought back to London from Oxford after the marriage, 'seems not much to have delighted in the pleasures of spare diet and hard study.' Within two months she had returned to her family in Oxfordshire, probably persuaded by her family, her mother in particular, promising to rejoin her husband by Michaelmas, but 'Milton was too busy to much miss his wife.' Michaelmas came and went with Mary showing 'no inclination to return to the sullen gloom of her husband's habitation, and therefore very willingly forgetting her promise.' By now Milton was becoming more than slightly irritated, especially as a succession of his letters remained unanswered and his messenger was rudely rebuffed. It was, however, a variety of other reasons that eventually persuaded Mary to return to the marital home: firstly, Milton dropped a few hints by publishing 'The Doctrine and Discipline of D-I-V-O-R-C-E', in which he mentioned the 'stepping to his neighbour's bed', something that may have been on his mind as he began to pay court to a Miss Davis; and secondly, the Civil War was by now raging and it was obvious to the Royalist Powell family that Milton, the staunch Parliamentarian, had backed the right side and they needed his protection. So after three years Mary returned, followed by the rest of her family: mother, father, three brothers and two sisters, who also moved into Milton's London home. The household, which already included various students of Milton's and his father, was further increased by the birth of John and Mary's first daughter, but the overcrowding was somewhat reduced when both their fathers died. The rest of the Powell brood stayed for about a year, after which Milton was able to move to a smaller house. For a man like Milton, who enjoyed his peace and quiet, the whole episode must have been a nightmare, quite apart from the fact that he never did get on well with her mother (she later sued him). Six years later Mary died in childbirth and Milton, now blind, was left to cope with three daughters. He married again, this time to Katherine Woodcock, who was his favourite wife, but she too died giving birth, losing the child, and 'her husband honoured her memory with a poor sonnet.' On the recommendation of a friend, Dr Paget, Milton married for a third time, this time to a cousin of Paget's, Elizabeth Minshull. It turned out to be rather a poor recommendation as she 'oppressed his children in his life-time, and cheated them at his death' by depriving them of their inheritance, selling the copyright of *Paradise Lost* for eight pounds. She survived Milton by 50 years.

MOLIÈRE
1622–1673

Molière's father had high hopes for the young Jean-Baptiste Poquelin. After all, he himself had made his way up in the world to become an Upholsterer to the King and a Royal valet. Just think of all those wonderful Louis Treize chairs that would need stuffing and all those marvellous tabards to be valeted, a good steady job for life with prospects. Jean-Baptiste had other ideas. (His father ended his life being supported by his prosperous son.) Encouraged by his grandfather, he fell in love with theatre and with an actress, Madeleine Béjart, who became his mistress. He abandoned the family name of Poquelin, adopted Molière as his stage name and set up his own theatre company in Paris. The troupe of actors, comprising several Béjarts including Madeleine, was conspicuously unsuccessful in presenting the fashionable tragedies of the day, and Molière was imprisoned for debt, released only when he was bailed out by his father. Unperturbed by this setback, Molière and Madeleine formed a new band of strolling players that roamed France for more than 10 years. Gradually they discovered that the comedies which Molière wrote were better received than the tragedies of Corneille and that the stuttering Molière, no tragedian, was a great comic actor. As they became more successful, the troupe was joined by two leading actresses, Mme du Parc and Mme de Brie. Molière fell wildly in love with the beautiful Mme du Parc, who signaled her complete rejection of him by marrying the fattest and ugliest actor in the company. This infatuation ended his relationship with Madeleine, who was replaced as his mistress by Mme de Brie, Molière's second choice for the part. The troupe was also joined by the ten-year-old Armande Béjart, who was introduced as Madeleine's youngest sister, although rumour had it that she was her daughter. After 12 nomadic years Molière and his actors returned to Paris in triumph under the patronage of King Louis XIV and his brother. Molière fell increasingly under the spell of Armande and when she was 20, they married. He was 40 and his jealous rivals in the Parisian theatre world, trying everything to discredit him, denounced Molière to the King, accusing him of marrying his own daughter. He survived this accusation, but the marriage was not a happy one with Armande more interested in Molière's young protégé, Michel Baron. During the fourth performance of *La Malade Imaginaire* (The Hypochondriac), Molière was taken violently ill and died later the same evening. It was a year to the day since Madeleine Béjart had died. He was buried in unconsecrated ground and when his death came to be recorded, his profession was entered as upholsterer and Royal valet.

WILLIAM MORRIS
1834–1896

The Pre-Raphaelite Brotherhood originally included the painters John Everett Millais and Henry Holman Hunt, and painter and poet Dante Gabriel Rossetti. Their aim was to inspire a return to art taken from nature and to move away from prevailing Victorian values. This loose association was later joined by William Morris and Edward Burne-Jones. They all had similar views on the ideal woman and all shared their models, with Rossetti's model and mistress, Lizzie Siddal, becoming Millais's *Ophelia*. Morris, Rossetti and Burne-Jones were all together in Oxford working on the frescoes of the Oxford Union when they first saw Jane Burden at the theatre. Both Rossetti and Morris fell madly in love with this latest 'stunner', who was to become the archetypal image of Pre-Raphaelite beauty. Rossetti was not married at the time, but felt under an obligation to marry the dying Lizzie Siddal. Frightened of losing Jane for himself and the Brotherhood, he persuaded her to marry Morris. He always seemed happy to defer to the wishes of Rossetti, the dominant figure in the group, and if he minded about the amount of time Jane and Rossetti spent together, then he suffered in silence. Rossetti also kept a menagerie to which he added an Indian bull because its eyes 'reminded him of Janey Morris'. After Lizzie's death, Jane became Rossetti's main model and inspiration. The three of them rented a country house in Oxfordshire, Kelmscott Manor, but the two men were rarely there at the same time. Jane, who always seemed ill, recovered dramatically in Morris's absence. Morris himself was drawn to Georgiana Burne-Jones, Edward's wife, but she remained totally indifferent. Morris and Rossetti eventually fell out over some financial matter and became completely estranged, probably to the great relief of Morris, but Jane continued to visit Rossetti until his death. When he died, she and Morris appeared to live contentedly, but after all that had gone before, who could be sure?

E. NESBIT
1858–1924

It seems to come as a bit of a surprise to find out that the author of that icon of childhood *The Railway Children* had a sex life at all, let alone a complicated marriage. When Edith Nesbit married Hubert Bland, she instantly acquired all that and more. Bland, a monocled, moustachioed Lothario, followed the precepts of free love as proposed by a fellow member of the Fabians, an early socialist group of which both he and Edith were founder members. Edith's best friend, Alice Hoatson, came to live with the Blands and promptly became Hubert's mistress. Hubert already had one illegitimate child by another mistress and Alice bore two more, who were adopted by Edith and brought up as part of the family. This *ménage à trois* continued until Hubert's death, with Alice always described as his 'secretary'. Edith got very keen on fellow Fabian George Bernard Shaw, whose rejection of her was his standard procedure with most women after encouraging their interest in the first place. Undiscouraged by that reverse, she began to have affairs with various young men as some sort of replacement for Hubert. After he died, Edith surprised everyone, including herself, by marrying the Captain of the Woolwich ferry, T.T. Tucker, and she went to live on Romney Marsh with 'The Skipper'.

OVID

43BC–AD18

Ovid was married first at 16, a union arranged for him by his family. It only seemed to last for two years, and later he was to refer to his first wife rather scathingly as '*nec dignis, nec utilis*'. For a single man, Rome in the early days of Augustus's reign was the place to be: there was a sexual revolution with women so emancipated that there were complaints that they, expected to be disloyal to their husbands, were even becoming disloyal to their lovers. Ovid's first book of poems, *Amores*, caught the mood and was an immediate and great success. There was a second marriage, again not for very long though possibly this time because of the death of his second wife, after which Ovid seemed to resume his philandering ways while researching his new book *Ars Amatoria*. Whereas *Amores* was about the innocence of young love, *Ars Amatoria* was a sophisticated guide to seduction and another bestseller. But the moral climate was changing, with the backlash starting in the Imperial family itself. The behaviour of Augustus's daughter, Julia, wife of his step-son and successor Tiberius, and of her daughter, another Julia, went beyond the bounds of even tolerated indecency with Julia the elder picking up a new lover every day in the Forum. She was exiled and denied all but specially approved male company, as too was Julia the younger. Somehow Ovid was drawn into this scandal, either directly in that he had been one of the Julias' lovers, or indirectly in that his poems, especially *Ars Amatoria*, had helped to corrupt Roman youth. Whatever the reason, he was exiled, not to some Mediterranean island like the Julias, but to one of the outer extremities of the Roman Empire, Tomis on the Black Sea. He had in the meantime married a third wife, but she did not share in his disgrace and exile and remained in Rome. For the last 10 years of his life Ovid desperately petitioned first Augustus, then Tiberius, to be allowed to return, but he never was and died in exile.

EDGAR ALLAN POE

1809–1849

Poe, the Jerry Lee Lewis of nineteenth-century America, married his 13-year-old cousin, Virginia Clemm. On the marriage licence she was described as 'of the full age of twenty-one years.' Born Edgar Poe into a theatrical family, he was orphaned by the time he was three and was brought up by a wealthy merchant, John Allan, in Richmond, Virginia. It was out of gratitude that he added 'Allan' to his name, yet he proved a grave disappointment to his adoptive family. His heavy drinking and gambling first showed themselves at university, from which his guardian withdrew him. Poe then enlisted in the army where for a while he led a fairly stable life, but it couldn't last and he was drummed out by court martial. Disowned by Allan, he went to Baltimore to the home of his father's sister, Maria Clemm, and joined the extended family that included his drunken consumptive brother Henry and his eight-year-old cousin Virginia. Periods of work were interspersed with Poe raving drunk, and one employer wrote in dismissing him: 'No man is safe who drinks before breakfast!' The pattern continued after his marriage to Virginia, with Mrs Clemm still in attendance to run the home, which was continually moving from Richmond and Baltimore to New York, to Philadelphia and back to New York as Poe was unable to hold down a job for any length of time or to make any money from his writing. While singing for friends one day, Virginia haemorrhaged, the scarlet stains that splashed her dress a vivid reminder of her tubercular condition. From that moment on her condition, always frail, worsened, not alleviated by the impoverished state of the family, and for the next five years until her death she was almost an invalid. When Virginia died, aged only 24, Poe was so heart-broken that he was often found weeping on Virginia's grave by Mrs Clemm, and he was so frightened of the dark that she had to sit with him every night until he fell asleep. Poe did recover sufficiently to consider liaisons with three female admirers, one of whom, Sarah Helen Whitman, broke off their engagement on receiving an anonymous letter warning her of 'this imprudent marriage'. Another was an old flame from Richmond, Elmira Shelton, to whom he was engaged at the time of his death. He was returning to New York to wind up his affairs via Baltimore, where, after disappearing for a week, he was found in the most desperate state lying in the gutter. Unable to account for his condition or the missing week, he was taken to the local hospital and survived only four days before he joined his beloved Virginia less than three years after she had died.

ALEXANDER PUSHKIN

1799–1837

The power of the written word has always seemed threatening to those who rule Russia, be they Tsars or Commissars, and both have always taken steps to curb it. For the father of modern Russian literature, this repression had fatal consequences. Pushkin managed to upset the authorities before he was 21 with his *Ode to Liberty*, and was exiled to his mother's estate in the country where the local functionaries were instructed to keep an eye on him, but they were unable to prevent the flow of seditious and blasphemous poems that Pushkin continued to produce anonymously. On his accession the new Tsar, Nicholas I, deciding that Pushkin needed closer supervision, summoned him to court, denied his request for foreign travel and appointed himself as the poet's censor. Not only did the Tsar have to approve all Pushkin's output, but the dreaded Third Section, Nicholas's forerunner of the KGB, also had to oversee everything that was published. Despite these interferences, Pushkin was soon seen as the people's champion against a repressive regime, and it was obvious to Nicholas and his henchmen that censorship was not sufficient to curtail this popularity. Pushkin, always renowned as a Don Juan around the court, had eventually married the most beautiful girl at court, Natalia Goncharova. Her beauty attracted many admirers, the most persistent among whom was the Baron d'Anthes, who, by chance, happened to be the best marksman in St Petersburg. Jealous that the naturally flirtatious Natalia encouraged such flattery, and goaded by some anonymous letters insinuating that her interest in the Baron went beyond the bounds of accepted propriety, Pushkin challenged him to a duel and was fatally wounded. When the news of Pushkin's death reached the masses, there was immediate suspicion about the circumstances and they came in their thousands to pay their respects. The authorities were so nervous that the body was smuggled away at night and buried secretly in some obscure monastery by members of the Third Section.

JEAN RHYS
1890–1979

She was born Ella Gwendolen Rees Williams on the West Indian island of Dominica, where she spent the first 17 years of her life. Her excitement at the prospect of going to England was soon replaced by disappointment and disillusion, heightened by her early career as a chorus girl with a third-rate company touring desolate Northern theatres. Life improved when she became the mistress of a wealthy stockbroker, Lancelot Hugh Smith, but his refusal to marry her and an abortion ended the affair. He continued to send her money until, at the end of the First World War, she met and married a Frenchman, Jean Lenglet, which was her passport to escape England. Even then, after they had settled in Paris, happiness eluded her. Their first child died of pneumonia and, when Lenglet was discovered embezzling, there followed several years on the run around Europe. When he was eventually caught and imprisoned, she turned to the writer Ford Madox Ford, with whom she had a brief affair. He encouraged her writing, chose her *nom de plume* of Jean Rhys and published her first pieces. With her marriage now over, she returned to London and for a while enjoyed a mildly successful literary career. She married again, this time to the stolid, dependable and dull Leslie Tilden Smith, and decided to revisit Dominica. The return reminded her of her arrival in England 30 years previously, bringing back the feelings of disenchantment and being made unwelcome. She never went back. She and Leslie barely existed as a couple; they fought, she drank and when Leslie died suddenly, her life with a third husband, Leslie's cousin Max Hamer, was actually worse. She thought Max was a respectable solicitor, but they both ended up in gaol, he for fraud and she for a drunken assault on a neighbour. She remained loyal to the disgraced Max with life made only just bearable by the generosity of his relations. Rediscovered when everyone thought she was dead, she started writing again and *The Wild Sargasso Sea* brought her late recognition at the age of 76, but not soon enough for Max, who died shortly before publication of the book.

JOHN WILMOT, EARL OF ROCHESTER

1647–1680

'If by chance then I wake, hot-headed and drunk,
What a coil do I make for the loss of my punk?
I storm, and I roar, and I fall in a rage,
And missing my lass, I bugger my page.'

Rochester, 'poet and libertine', is better remembered today as the latter, although his occasional activity as the former entitles him to a place in this book. At the age of 18 he kidnapped, from under the nose of her grandfather, the heiress Elizabeth Mallet, to replenish his already diminished fortune. Imprisoned in the Tower for this 'High Misdemeanour', Rochester was soon released, as befitted one of King Charles II's favourites. This favouritism proved useful in extracting him from various escapades, although Charles's patience did wear thin when he was the butt of Rochester's lampoons. After distinguishing himself in the Wars against the Dutch, Rochester returned to court, married Elizabeth Mallet and 'then unhappily addicted himself to dissolute and vicious company' and 'pursued low amours in mean disguises'. He adopted these disguises when he had been banished from court, and the adventures that they occasioned were always designed to amuse the King and gain his forgiveness, which invariably they did. In one episode he and the Duke of Buckingham, in disgrace together, ran an inn near Newmarket, got the husbands drunk and seduced the wives. Another time Rochester set himself up as a doctor and astrologer called 'Alexander Bendo', specialising in dispensing quack potions and advice to women on how to improve their appearance, another foolproof source of seducees. But in the major love of his life, the actress Elizabeth Barry, he met his match. After he helped launch her career she promptly dropped him, a rare reverse for Rochester. His 'ostentatious contempt of regularity' and syphilis had done for him by the time he was 30, having 'blazed out his youth and his health in lavish voluptuousness', and at 32 he was dead.

DANTE GABRIEL ROSSETTI

1828–1882

On the night of 5 October 1869 there gathered a strange group round a fire in Highgate cemetery in London. There were grave-diggers, cemetery officials, lawyers, doctors, someone from the Home Office and Charles Augustus Howell. They were all there to disinter the body of Dante Gabriel Rossetti's wife, Lizzie Siddal, buried seven years previously. The only absentee was Rossetti himself: all the arrangements had been made by the enigmatic Howell

who made himself indispensable in turn to Ruskin, Rossetti and Swinburne. For Rossetti, models were also mistresses. Lizzie Siddal was the most long-standing, the original Pre-Raphaelite inspiration and Millais' 'Ophelia'. She and Fanny Cornforth, 'The Elephant', alternated in Rossetti's affection. He then fell desperately in love with Jane Burden, whom he met at the theatre with William Morris, Edward Burne-Jones and Arthur Hughes. When Jane decided to marry Morris, Rossetti married Lizzie 10 years too late. Never the strongest of women, her delicate consumptive appearance had nonetheless been one of her great attractions, but, by the time of their marriage, Lizzie was dying. Less than two years later she was dead from an overdose of laudanum, probably knowingly taken. As an act of contrition the remorseful Rossetti consigned the manuscript of his latest poems to the grave with Lizzie. It was seven years later when he changed his mind and recovered his disinfected manuscript, the exhumation of which he had hoped would remain secret. Howell's indiscretion scotched that hope and the attendant publicity did no harm to the sale of the poems. For the rest of his life Rossetti found solace with Jane Morris, particularly when her husband took his trips to Iceland, but continued use of chloral reduced him to a shell of his former self and led to his early death.

JOHN RUSKIN
1819–1900

Ruskin's knowledge of the female form was limited to his study of Classical sculpture and it came as a great surprise to him, when he saw his wife naked on the first night of their honeymoon, to discover that she had pubic hair. The prospect so unnerved and disgusted him that the marriage remained unconsummated. His first love had been Adèle Domecq, daughter of his father's partner in a wine

and sherry company, a union that might have been good for business had not Adèle been the subject of an arranged marriage to a French Baron. Instead Ruskin married Euphemia Gray, whose knowledge of 'the duties of married persons' was as limited as his. He was 29, she 19, so perhaps her ignorance was more excusable than his. Among his other reasons for non-consummation was his 'hatred to children' and his anxiety 'that my wife should be well and strong in order that she might be able to climb Swiss hills with me that year. I had seen much grief arise from the double excitement of possession and marriage travelling.' Effie, as she was known, remained unpossessed for five years. Ruskin's championship of the Pre-Raphaelite painters led to a friendship with John Everett Millais, who accompanied the Ruskins on a painting holiday in Scotland. The result was Millais' famous portrait of Ruskin by a waterfall and Effie and Millais falling in love. As Millais' brother, William, who was also there, was later to recall 'I may say that I think Ruskin did not act wisely in putting JEM and ECG continually together . . . a very dangerous experiment.' Ruskin was totally oblivious to what was happening and was greatly shocked when Effie deserted him. Their marriage was soon annulled on the grounds of Ruskin's 'incurable impotency' and Effie was declared, after appropriate medical inspection, a *virgo intacta*. She and Millais were married within the year. Ruskin bore Millais no ill-will, indeed he seemed positively relieved and more interested in his portrait than his wife. Elizabeth Carlyle wrote to a friend 'I never saw a man so improved by the loss of his wife.' Ruskin had one more infatuation, this time with Rose La Touche, but perhaps mindful of Effie, he retired to a bachelor existence in the Lakes. Effie and Millais had a most happy marriage and she produced eight children.

GEORGE SAND

1804–1876

George Sand, the '*sans culotte*' of nineteenth-century French literature, cut a swathe through Parisian society on her belated arrival in the capital. Christened Lucille-Aurore Dupin, she spent the first 10 years of her adult life in the country as the wife of a boring retired Army officer, Casimir Dudevant, bringing up two children. Her persistent demands for a life of independence were suddenly and surprisingly approved by Casimir and off she went to Paris to pursue the life of a writer. Her first book was a collaboration with Jules Sandeau, published under the *nom de plume* of Jules Sand, half of which she was to adopt. Her first notorious liaison was with the spoilt, idle, but brilliant poet Alfred de Musset. They set off on a tour of Italy, where first she became seriously ill in Genoa and then in Venice he was struck down. While she was ill, de Musset had amused himself with the local women; while he was ill, she nursed him assiduously, but unfortunately there was a rather handsome Italian doctor, Pietro Pagello, in attendance as well. She and Pietro started an affair and when de Musset, physically recovered, returned to Paris, she remained in Venice. She brought her handsome young doctor back to Paris, got bored with him, sent him home and took up again for a few final tempestuous months with de Musset. Various other affairs followed, often with the famous, including Frédéric Chopin and Prosper Mérimée. Once, when she was having a row with her son-in-law, a sculptor, she threatened to publish the details: he, in turn, threatened to do a carving of her arse which, he said, everybody in Paris would recognise.

WILLIAM SHAKESPEARE

1564–1616

*'A woman's face, with Nature's own hand painted,
Hast thou, the Master Mistress of my passion.'*

The mystery of Mr W.H., the dedicatee and 'onlie be-getter' of Shakespeare's sonnets, has kept scholars and literary sleuths busy for centuries. Some have plumped for aristocrats such as William Herbert, the Earl of Pembroke, or Henry Wriothesley, Earl of Southampton, others for mere commoners such as William Hughes, William Hall, William Hathaway or William Hatcliffe, but the answer is closer to home. Homosexuality was rife in the Elizabethan theatre, hardly surprising with all the female parts being written for and played by young boys. Shakespeare was obviously not immune to the attractions of boy-actors, like his contemporary and fellow playwright Christopher Marlowe; but the man in his life was not an actor. William Hart worked backstage for the Lord Chamberlain's company as a costumier. He had been an 'unperfect' actor as a boy, taking the female roles, but when his voice broke he was unable to make the transition to the adult male roles, his effeminacy being the major obstacle. Shakespeare, who had been forced into marriage at 18 to the already pregnant Anne Hathaway, eight years his senior, was by this time in love with William, and in order to keep him in the company had him taken on as a costumier in charge of hats. Even this was not sufficiently close enough for Shakespeare, who per-suaded his sister Joan to marry William, and when Shakespeare retired to Stratford-upon-Avon, so too did William. It is known that on his return to Stratford Shakespeare was not very popular with the locals, and perhaps the reason was his blatant relationship with William. After all, what was acceptable in Blackfriars was not so readily condoned in Warwickshire. When William Hart died, Shakespeare was so 'heartbroken' that within the week he too was dead. In his will all that Shakespeare left his wife was his 'second-best' bed, a calculated insult, while William's widow Joan and her family fared much better. As to the identity of 'The Dark Lady' of the Sonnets, perhaps William Hart took to marriage and his wife far more than Shakespeare had anticipated and it was Joan who was the 'Dark Lady', the woman who came between the poet and his true love — or perhaps we are no nearer the truth than before.

PERCY BYSSHE SHELLEY

1792–1822

A trail of disasters followed Shelley throughout his life like some avenging angel, starting with his expulsion from Oxford for blasphemy and continuing with his first marriage. His first wife, Harriet Westbrook, was only 16 when she and the 19-year-old Shelley eloped to Scotland. After the marriage they were joined first by his best friend Thomas Hogg, who always fancied Shelley's women, and then by Harriet's elder sister, Eliza, who cordially disliked her new brother-in-law. Shelley always had problems with his sisters-in-law. Never settled anywhere for long, the Shelleys lived for a while at a commune in Bracknell, Berkshire, where Percy's main interest was a French vegetarian, Cornelia Boinville. This weakened the already tenuous marriage, which finally collapsed when Shelley met Mary Godwin. In pursuit of his political ideals, Shelley had written to Mary's father William Godwin, the radical novelist and philosopher, to introduce himself, and in time became part of Godwin's extended household. He fell violently in love with Mary, Godwin's daughter by his first wife, Mary Wollstonecraft, one of the first feminists and author of *The Rights of Women*, but unknown to him both Fanny Imlay, Mary's half-sister, and Claire Clairmont, Mary's step-sister, had fallen in love with him. He eloped for a second time, this time with the two 16-year-olds, Mary and Claire, and set off for Europe. The deserted Harriet was four months pregnant. She still held out hopes of a reconciliation when he returned, but even the imminent birth of his child failed to move Shelley and anyway Mary was by now pregnant as well. His insensitivity and callousness was to have tragic consequences. First Fanny, her infatuation for Shelley unrequited, took an overdose of laudanum and then Harriet, abandoned by Shelley, drowned herself in the Serpentine. With these two deaths on his conscience, Shelley went into self-imposed exile in Italy with Mary, now his second wife, and with, as usual, Claire, now Byron's mistress. Shelley was not long in provoking Mary to jealousy by his involvement with a young Italian, Emilia Viviani, and with Jane Williams, wife of a friend. It was with Jane's husband, Edward, that Shelley took his fateful journey in the Gulf of Spezzia, where their boat was sunk by a sudden storm and both were drowned. The widowed Jane, Shelley's last love, returned to England where she became Hogg's wife, thus completing the circle.

SOCRATES

469–399 BC

Not a lot is known about the married life of Socrates, except that his wife, Xanthippe, was a bit of a shrew. She may, of course, have had good reason, as he was known to prefer boys and promoted homosexual love as the highest aspiration for every right-thinking man, and love between man and woman only good for producing children. Although this may have been the accepted view among the literati of the day, unfortunately the Athenian authorities had other ideas. Socrates was brought to trial for espousing new Gods and corrupting the Athenian youth. He was found guilty and condemned to death. Attempts were made by his friends to organise his escape, but he refused and met his fate by the drinking of hemlock with great courage and dignity.

ROBERT SOUTHEY

1775–1843

Like Dickens, Southey married the wrong sister. As the leader of a group of young radical idealists, the Pantisocrats, who were planning to set-up a Utopian commune on the banks of the Susquehanna in Pennsylvania, Southey felt that it was his duty to provide his fellow Utopians, poets Samuel Taylor Coleridge and Robert Lovell, with suitable wives. The unfortunate women chosen were three Bristol sisters, Edith, Sara and Mary Fricker; Southey kept Edith for himself and Coleridge was alloted Sara and Lovell Mary. Coleridge had to be cajoled into marrying Sara, the union was a disaster, and when Coleridge deserted her, Southey was left supporting Sara and Coleridge's family. As he had always felt that he had married the wrong sister and much preferred Sara, her arrival in his household remedied the situation. They were all joined eventually by the widowed third sister and Southey, like Wordsworth, seemed perfectly content with his three 'wives'. To maintain his extended family Southey had to work unceasingly, abandoning the radical ideals of his youth to such an extent that he was made Poet Laureate in preference to his contemporary Wordsworth. At the end of her life Edith went mad, perhaps unable to cope with the overcrowded household, and was wheeled off to the asylum at York, where she died. Southey, now free to marry Sara, surprised everyone, especially Sara, by going off and marrying an admiring bluestocking, Caroline Bowles. Perhaps he had had enough of the Frickers.

STENDHAL
1783–1842

The first impression that everyone had of Henri Beyle, better known under his *nom de plume* of Stendhal, was of a rather inconsequential buffoon, but when they discovered that he was a great lover, the second impression was one of amazement. Stendhal's whole life was spent in the worship and pursuit of women — '*La Chasse du Bonheur*' – and from his first adolescent infatuation with a touring actress in his home town of Grenoble to his death he was always in love. Sometimes these affairs were only '*l'amour de tête*', but that was sufficient for Stendhal to add them to his list of successful conquests which he kept on his braces. Being a fat man he had big braces which is just as well considering the number of mistresses he amassed during his lifetime. He also wrote a book *De l'Amour*, in which he enumerated the four different kinds of love: *l'amour physique*, *l'amour goût*, *l'amour de vanité* and *l'amour passion*, though strangely enough not *l'amour de tête*. Stendhal's own *amours* were of course always '*l'amour passion*'. When his initial attempts at seduction proved fruitless, he got a successful friend to write down his technique and in all his future affairs Stendhal followed these instructions to the letter, with great and surprising success. On one occasion his attempts to be inconspicuous in the quest for a certain lady were particularly laughable, with his disguise comprising green spectacles and an orange wig which made him look like either a plump pantomime clown or a corpulent caricature of Robespierre. He also always wore his best striped trousers for the expected triumphal moment of seduction. It does seem greatly to his credit that he always seemed to realise what a ludicrous sight he presented to the world and that he never took himself too seriously. Slights, rejections and disappointments, and there were many, never put him off and though he never found Mlle Droit and had to be content with his numerous mistresses, he seemed to achieve his ambitions and live up to his epitaph:

Visse, scrisse, amo.

LYTTON STRACHEY

1880–1932

On a cold February day in 1909 a solitary man was to be seen making his way across London for some strange reason best known to himself. Giles Lytton Strachey was about to propose to Virginia Stephen, and for some still stranger reason she was about to accept. Lytton, having idealised her elder brother Thoby, and now upset that Maynard Keynes had taken Duncan Grant from him, decided that it was about time he left home and that marriage to Virginia was the answer. They both immediately realised that they had made a dreadful mistake and Strachey wrote to his friend Leonard Woolf in Ceylon suggesting that he marry Virginia instead. Various unsatisfactory affairs followed for Lytton, until he met Dora Carrington, a young painter. Carrington, as she was always known, was then having an affair with Mark Gertler, another painter, to whom Strachey was also attracted. After Strachey had supplanted Gertler in Carrington's affections, she and Lytton stayed together through a complicated merry-go-round of sexual partners until he died. The *ménage* was never less than *à trois*, more commonly *à quatre* and often more. The androgynous Carrington always attracted men who appealed to Lytton and whose sexual favours were a source of competition between them. The first of these was Ralph Partridge, who did marry Carrington, the next Gerald Brenan. Lytton always had his own supply of young men and seemed to view the goings-on around him with amused tolerance. When Ralph fell in love with Frances Marshall and Gerald Brenan returned to Spain, Lytton and Carrington were thrown together once more and it was their relationship, which appeared the most unlikely, that proved the strongest. As Lytton lay dying, Carrington tried to commit suicide by inhaling car exhaust fumes in a locked garage. Discovered in time by Ralph, she succeeded at the second attempt within two months of Lytton's death, this time with a shotgun.

AUGUST STRINDBERG

1849–1912

Strindberg had a major problem as far as women were concerned: he was terrified of them. Perhaps by marrying three times he was trying some primitive form of aversion therapy. His first marriage, to Siri von Essen, started well enough, but Strindberg became insanely jealous

of her dog and her maid, the former for no good reason as far as we know, but the latter for very good reason because Siri became a lesbian. She left August in Sweden to live with Marie David, a Dane, in Finland. Strindberg's play, *The Father*, with its bitter tone and its misogyny, was the product of the breakdown of his first marriage. It was while in Berlin that he met his second wife, Frida Uhl, an Austrian writer and literary groupie. Their marriage lasted less than a year. Strindberg was the first of her conquests, Frank Wedekind, the German playwright, the second, and others included Wyndham Lewis and Augustus John, who actually found Frida more than even he could handle. In times of depression, especially after the collapse of his marriages, Strindberg turned to the occult and to dabbling in alchemy, searching unsuccessfully for the Philosopher's Stone to turn base metals into gold. This undermined his health, both physical and mental, with his body being covered with suppurating sores from the sulphur he used and with his mind becoming totally unhinged. Strindberg had a history of mental instability with early attempts at suicide, but now serious paranoia took hold and he imagined being pursued at various times by all the world's feminists, the population of Sweden and all London's beggars disguised as giants. He went mad. He recovered sufficiently on his return to Sweden to marry a Norwegian actress, Harriet Bosse, for whom he wrote several parts. Even this was not enough to keep them together and within a couple of years they had parted. However, in his final years Strindberg did find some sort of stability when he received the literary recognition which he had always craved.

JONATHAN SWIFT

1667–1745

*'Cleanliness in the first and competence
in the second is all I look for.'*

There were two Esthers in Swift's life, Esther Johnson —
'Stella' — and Esther Vanhomrigh — 'Vanessa', a
strange coincidence, for the use of the name was then, as
now, fortunately rare. He first met Esther Johnson when he
worked as secretary to Sir William Temple, a famous
politician of the day. Stella was supposedly the daughter of
Temple's steward, but may have been his illegitimate child.
She and her friend Mrs Rebecca Dingley (The Mrs or
Mistress in those days did not imply married status, merely
that you were too old to be a Miss) were persuaded by Swift
to move to Ireland to be near him. He had been born in
Dublin and his life alternated between Ireland and England.
His *Journal to Stella* is an account to the two women of four
years spent in England until his appointment as Dean of St
Patrick's Cathedral, Dublin in 1713. It was during this stay
in England that he met the second Esther, for whom he
invented the name Vanessa, and Swift was of an age when
his 'vanity was strongly excited by the amorous attention of
a young woman.' She was also induced to come and live in
Ireland with her mother, but under what hope we cannot
know, only that it must have been false. For Stella had
accepted Swift's modest proposal of marriage and they were
secretly married, although their lives remained unchanged
and they continued to live in separate houses, Swift having
'annexed the expectation of all the pleasures of perfect
friendship, without the uneasiness of conjugal restraint. She
was never treated as a wife, and to the world she had the
appearance of a mistress.' As Lord Orrery, a friend, wrote:
'It would be difficult to prove that they were ever afterwards
together without a third person', and Vanessa remained
totally oblivious to the marriage, although Swift saw her
less and less and she became more and more 'splenetic' and

unhappy. When she died young, some said of a broken heart, Swift's poem 'Cadenus and Vanessa' about their relationship was published by someone keen to discredit the Dean, by now an important and powerful figure in Ireland. The publication greatly distressed Stella, unaware of the younger Esther, but she put on a brave front. When someone ignorant of her closeness to Swift remarked that Vanessa must have been an extraordinary woman to have inspired the Dean to write so finely, Stella replied that on the contrary, 'It was well known that the Dean could write finely upon a broomstick.' Stella died, still disappointed that Swift never publicly acknowledged her as his wife, and 'his benevolence was contracted, and his severity exasperated.'

WILLIAM MAKEPEACE THACKERAY
1811–1863

Thackeray had for a mother-in-law the archetypal example, the one that gives the breed a bad name, and her influence was so detrimental that she was responsible for the history of insanity that permeated the family. Mrs Shawe disapproved of her daughter Isabella's marriage to Thackeray in the first place, perhaps understandably as he was at the time a struggling, penniless artist and writer in Paris. Despite the mother's dominant personality, which had left her daughters simpering wrecks, the marriage was initially very happy with Isabella greatly changed away from her mother. Within four years, however, Isabella, distraught at the death of a second daughter, was completely unhinged by the birth of a third and went mad. On a boat trip to Ireland to see her mother she threw herself overboard and fortunately was rescued, but her mother refused to put her and Thackeray up as she said it would be bad for her nerves. On their return to Paris Isabella was committed to a French asylum and became one of the many mad women of Chaillot. Thackeray eventually brought her back to London, where she was looked after by friends, but she never recovered her senses and he saw her less and less. By now, following the publication of *Vanity Fair*, he had become rich and famous, and yet he lived a rather lonely and solitary life with his daughters, his only consolation an unconsummated passion for Jane Brookfield, the wife of an old friend. In one of his drawings Thackeray portrays himself as her lapdog, which he remained until her husband, a disappointed cleric, finally objected to his persistent presence. The quietly mad Isabella survived him by 30 years.

COUNT LEO TOLSTOY

1828–1910

The Moscow Express had been cancelled, and the station-master at Astapovo was trying to placate irate passengers. He was also rather keen to have his own office back to himself and escape the hordes of journalists and photographers from all over the world who had invaded his tiny railway station on the Russian steppes: they had arrived expecting to record the final reconciliation between the dying Leo Tolstoy and his wife Sonya, who was coming from Yasnaya Polyana on a specially chartered train. At the age of 82, and after 48 increasingly bitter years of marriage, Tolstoy had run away from home, only to collapse with pneumonia at Astapovo station, allowing Sonya time to catch up with him. She had been only 18 when they married, whereas Tolstoy, at 34, had sowed several acres of wild oats before deciding the time was right to settle down. He had paid court to the three daughters of Dr Behrs and was expected to marry the eldest, Liza, although he really had his eye on the youngest, Tatyana. In the end he surprised everyone by proposing to Sonya, the middle one and the plainest. She accepted and they married a week later. On their wedding night he raped her on the way back to his estate at Yasnaya Polyana. It shouldn't have come as much of a shock to Sonya, as before the wedding he had insisted that she read his diaries, which recorded in intimate detail all his previous love affairs. After that first night, the early years of the marriage passed contentedly enough, with Tolstoy completing *War and Peace*, (although it was Tatyana Behrs, not Sonya, he used as the model for Natasha). Gradually Tolstoy's interest in new fads and philosophies led to an estrangement between him and Sonya, especially when, in the case of his belief in no sex even within marriage, he didn't practise what he preached. Sonya was continually pregnant — they had 13 children — and Tolstoy carried on much as before, exercising his *droit de seigneur* over various peasants and serfs, particularly Aksinya Bazykina. This is probably the reason that Tolstoy took to wearing peasant dress: so that he didn't pick up the wrong clothes in the dark. When Sonya fell for the composer Sergey Tanayev and followed him everywhere, Tolstoy, of course, issued her with an ultimatum: him or me. They both became totally paranoid about each other's behaviour, until his obsession culminated in his flight and eventual death in the station-master's office in Astapovo. All those journalists and photographers never did get their story, as Sonya was only admitted to his death-bed after Tolstoy had sunk into his final coma.

IVAN TURGENEV

1818–1883

Turgenev's story is about one of the great unrequited loves of all time. It lasted for 40 years, nearly all his adult life. It was in St Petersburg in 1843 that Turgenev met Pauline Viardot Garcia, a Spanish opera singer and wife of a middle-aged French writer, Louis Viardot. Whether the affair remained solely platonic or was eventually consummated seems not to be known for sure, but it dragged Turgenev all over Europe to be nearer Pauline from the moment he met her until he died. For the last 20 years of his life he lived with the Viardots as part of the family, first in Baden Baden and finally in Paris, only visiting Russia for a short period every year. He seemed to get on equally well with Monsieur Viardot as with Pauline, and he even brought his illegitimate daughter (by one of his family servants) to live in the Viardot household. His involuntary exile, however, affected his work, and all his best writing was done while he was still living in Russia. His mother, a battleaxe of the first order, cut his allowance because of his liaison with Pauline. He went through paroxysms of jealousy over an affair that she had with a painter who was doing her portrait, especially as within a year she had had a son. That led to one of the many break-ups that punctuated their relationship, but as usual they made up. As Turgenev said, if the Viardots had gone to Australia, he would have followed. His dog-like infatuation made Turgenev the most cosmopolitan of Russian writers, friend of Flaubert, Zola and Thackeray as well as Gogol and Tolstoy. Even when her husband died, Pauline refused to marry him, though she was at his bedside when he died in Paris. He was buried in Russia, where 100,000 people attended the funeral. Pauline described him as '*le plus triste des hommes*'.

LOPE DE VEGA

1562–1635

Plays, poems, novels and women dominated the life of Spanish playwright Lope de Vega, and it is a wonder that the writing and the women were not mutually exclusive. A lifetime's output of 1,500 plays, numerous poems and a couple of novels makes his contemporaries Shakespeare and Cervantes look like non-starters. His first love affair led to the premature end of his university career, so he took himself off to Madrid, became immersed in the theatre and fell in love with the wife of Spain's leading actor. When her mother stopped the affair — not because she was cuckolding her husband, but because she had the opportunity to become the mistress of someone more wealthy and influential — he lampooned the whole family in verse. For this he was imprisoned and exiled from Madrid on pain of death. Even this threat was insufficient to prevent him from returning to seduce the aristocratic Isabel de Urbina, although they had to be married by proxy since he was not supposed to be in Madrid. Before married life could begin, the Armada intervened and Lope de Vega was one of the fortunate few who returned unscathed from the attempted invasion of England, also managing to compose an 11,000-line poem on the trip. Six years of stable married life with Isabel followed, but when she died, he married in Toledo one Juana de Guardo, apparently for money rather than love, the latter being catered for in Madrid by an actress, Micaela de Lujan. After the death of Juana, he decided on a new career in his fifties and rather surprisingly opted for the church, which even more surprisingly ordained him. Within two years he had fallen in love with a married woman, Marta de Nevares Santoyo, by whom he had a daughter, and had predictably renounced holy orders. When her husband died, she and Lope lived together, but tragedy intervened. She first went blind, then mad, and died. Their daughter was kidnapped and seduced by a young blood, an all too familiar event from Lope's past, but this time, with him as the wronged parent, it was sufficient to break his heart and kill him.

PAUL VERLAINE

1844–1896
(RIMBAUD TOO)

The lives of the two French poets Paul Verlaine and
Arthur Rimbaud (1854–1891) are inextricably linked,
and the destruction of Verlaine's life was due to Rimbaud's
evil genius. Rimbaud was a poetic prodigy who sent some of
his early work to Verlaine for approval. On the strength of
them, Verlaine invited him to Paris. Rimbaud was a month
short of his seventeenth birthday when he arrived. The
effect of their meeting on Verlaine was catastrophic for him
and his family: he threw up his job, he deserted his wife and
young son and joined Rimbaud in a dissipated life of drink

and drugs in the Latin Quarter. Verlaine's mother accused Rimbaud, 10 year his junior, of corrupting her son — and she was right. Rimbaud returned home to allow Verlaine and his wife a chance of a reconciliation, but Verlaine found that he could not live without his young friend and implored him to return. They left Paris, going first to Brussels and then London, where their pursuit of the low-life continued, this time with opium added to the menu. It was after they returned to Brussels that the infamous shooting took place: Verlaine, drunk as usual, quarrelled with Rimbaud, produced a gun and fired two shots. Rimbaud was wounded, not seriously, in the wrist, and Verlaine was sentenced to two years in a Belgian gaol. It was the end of the '*drôle de ménage*', which probably came as a relief to Rimbaud as he was fed up with the cling-on Verlaine had become. Their relationship had lasted less than two years and Verlaine's life was damaged beyond repair. After his release from prison Verlaine's vagabond existence followed a desultory pattern of teaching and farming. The sudden tragic death of another young companion, Lucien Letinois, whose attraction was that he reminded Verlaine of Rimbaud, led to a mental breakdown, followed by another spell in prison for attacking his aged mother. Verlaine spent his final years in Paris drunk and destitute, while Rimbaud became a gun-runner and slave-trader in Aden, his literary life all but forgotten.

EDMUND WALLER

1606–1687

By the time he was 25, Waller was a wealthy widower and paying court to Lady Dorothea Sidney, the eldest daughter of the Earl of Leicester. She became the 'Sacharissa' of his poems, the name implying, as Dr Johnson notes, 'a spiritless mildness, and dull goodness, such as excites rather tenderness than esteem, and such as, though always treated with kindness, is never honoured or admired.' Waller thought her 'a sublime predominating beauty, of lofty charms and imperious influence', but his flattery was insufficient to win her love and she disdainfully rejected him to marry an Earl. On her wedding day Waller wrote to her sister invoking various curses on Lady Dorothea's head, including 'On one who is so silent, the noise of children and, on one who is so fair, the great curse of old age.' As for the former, we do not know how many children Lady Dorothea may have had, although we do know that Waller's second wife bore him 13 children, so perhaps Dorothea made a wise decision in rejecting him. Regarding the second half of the curse, Waller may have derived some satisfaction. They did meet again in old age and when she asked whether he would write similar verses to her again, he replied: 'When you are as young, Madam, and as handsome as you were then.'

EVELYN WAUGH

1903–1966

Evelyn (f): Old German Avelina introduced as Aveline into England by the Normans; common in the twelfth and thirteenth centuries, giving rise to surnames Aveling and Evelyn.
Evelyn (m): as a man's name this seems to date only from the seventeenth century and to be derived from the surname Evelyn.

Perhaps the critic in the *Times Literary Supplement* who ascribed Evelyn Waugh's first book to a 'Miss Waugh' could be forgiven his confusion, as even after 300 years Evelyn as a man's name was somewhat rare, although a typically astringent Waugh letter upbraided him for 'his limited social experience'. Any confusion was compounded when Waugh fell in love and married Evelyn Gardner, who became known to their friends as She-Evelyn to his He-Evelyn. Fortunately for all concerned, this distinction was short-lived as after a year the She-Evelyn ran off. Constancy had never been one of her strong points, since she had already broken off three previous engagements before their marriage. She confessed that the only reason for wedding in the first place was to escape a particularly domineering mother. Disillusioned and embittered, Waugh turned to the Catholic Church for consolation, a decision that was to prove a major obstacle when he wished to remarry. When he set about having his first marriage annulled on the grounds that he and the She-Evelyn had not entered into it in a serious spirit, he found that the ecclesiastical courts were exceeding slow. It was only after four years and numerous expensive lunches for leading Catholic luminaries that he was free to marry Laura Herbert, a cousin of the She-Evelyn, which provoked one aged Herbert aunt to remark: 'I thought we'd heard the last of that young man!'

H.G. WELLS
1866–1946

Apart from Balzac, it would be difficult to imagine a more unlikely literary Casanova than Wells. He was short, tubby, rather unprepossessing to look at with an incongruously high-pitched voice, and yet he had a list of amorous conquests to rival Don Juan. He started off conventionally

enough, marrying his cousin Isabel, but soon ran off with one of his students from the college where he taught after a consumptive attack induced him to think that he was about to die. He survived for another 53 years. His second wife, Amy Catherine Robbinns, Wells rechristened, for some reason best known himself, Jane, and although the marriage survived, in name anyway, for 32 years until her death, his disillusion with her was almost instantaneous and it was only Jane's forebearance of Wells's philandering that maintained the charade. This time his first extra-marital affair was his attempted rape of Isabel, the failure of which led to his complete mental breakdown for several months. As an espouser of free love and a leading light in the Fabian Society, Wells was able to combine both pursuits with various ardent young socialist women, though E. Nesbit managed to rescue her daughter from his clutches on Paddington Station. Amber Reeves, who was the most long-standing of these Fabian relationships, was followed by Rebecca West among his succession of mistresses, and both had sons by him. Rebecca West had met Wells when she was invited to stay after a hostile review of one of his books, inappropriately called *Marriage*. Arnold Bennett described his old friend Wells as 'a wonder of energy: four novels a year, five mistresses all over the country every year — a regular juggler.' Old age didn't seem to lessen his stamina either as a writer or as a lover, a dual career which he continued to the end.

VIRGINIA WOOLF

1882–1941

The fumbling sexual advances of her elder half-brother, George Duckworth, who also tried the same tactics with her sister Vanessa, may be what put Virginia Woolf off sex. They may also be the reason why she initially accepted a proposal of marriage from Lytton Strachey. Both then thought better of it; 'an awkward moment' and 'repulsive' were the words Strachey used to describe the incident, and

they disengaged themselves. It was probably a wise decision, although, with his known preferences and her frigidity, it might have been the ideal match and would certainly have been the literary match of the day. It was Strachey who wrote to his friend Leonard Woolf suggesting that he return from Ceylon and marry Virginia, which in time he did. Marriage to Leonard did not seem to improve her already delicate health, particularly her mental health, which deteriorated to such an extent that she suffered various breakdowns, culminating in an attempted suicide a year after they married. Virginia was also attracted to strong, formidable women who stirred ambivalent, though normally unrequited, feelings within her. Before her marriage it had been Violet Dickinson; after, there was first Katherine Mansfield and then Vita Sackville West. It was with the 'Sapphist' Vita that Virginia had her most passionate and requited affair, one that started with Vita enthralled and ended with Virginia desolate. The sex-changing character Orlando in Virginia's book of the same name is based on Vita Sackville West, and ironically it was this book, hastily written in a more lighthearted vein than usual, that proved to be her first real success. The next *dame formidable* was the ancient, deaf composer Ethel Smyth, but for this last affair there was passion without physical involvement. The return of symptoms that she knew presaged madness prompted another suicide bid, this time successful.

WILLIAM WORDSWORTH

1770–1850

'Mr Robinson says he never saw a man so happy in three wives as Mr Wordsworth is.' So wrote Mary Lamb to one of Wordsworth's 'wives', Sarah Hutchinson, sister of his actual wife, Mary. The third 'wife' was Dorothy Wordsworth, the poet's sister, who was so close to William that on his wedding day she became hysterical, took to her bed and refused to attend the service. It was one of the few times in their lives that brother and sister were parted, but it had happened once before. In 1792 Wordsworth went to France alone to see for himself the effects of the Revolution, and in Orléans he had met and fallen in love with Annette Vallon, but, as conditions between England and France deteriorated, he was unable to stay for the birth of their daughter Caroline later that same year. The affair remained totally secret outside the confines of the family for over a hundred years, until it was unearthed by a French scholar in 1920. After the Peace of Amiens in 1802 Wordsworth was able to visit France again to meet his daughter for the first time, but not alone, as on this visit he was chaperoned by Dorothy. It was immediately on his return from Paris that he married Mary Hutchinson. After the marriage all three, William, Mary and Dorothy, lived in Dove Cottage at Grasmere in the Lake District, where they were later to be joined by Sarah Hutchinson to complete the *ménage*. Dorothy wrote in her diary: 'Wm fell asleep, lying on my breast and I upon Mary.' Where Sarah was at the time is not recorded. When Wordsworth's publishers went through his papers after his death, they found a lot of unprintable erotic poetry, which prompted George Meredith to remark, 'The poet of the cathedral aisle, once outside, kicks like a goat.'

WILLIAM WYCHERLEY

1640–1716

Wycherley's first play 'Love in A Wood' brought fame and a rather surprising introduction to Charles II's mistress Barbara Villiers, Duchess of Cleveland, she of 'the boundless appetite' who 'sinn'd for exercise'. While he was driving down Pall Mall, a lady leaned out of her carriage and called out, 'You, Wycherley, you are the son of a whore!' Momentarily taken aback, Wycherley realised that she was alluding to a quote in his play and turned in pursuit. When he had caught her up, he recognised the famous beauty and invited her to his play at Drury Lane. She accepted and sat in the front row while 'Mr Wycherley in the pit under her entertained her during the whole play.' This was the start of an affair that 'made a great noise in the Town'. When Wycherley did eventually marry, it was to another aristocrat, the widowed Countess of Drogheda, daughter of the Earl of Radnor. But Wycherley's absence from court in pursuit of the widow so displeased Charles II that he lost the job as tutor to one of the king's bastard sons, though not one of the three that Barbara Villiers bore. The widow proved to be an extremely jealous wife, who prevented his return to court and generally kept a close eye on him. Wycherley was in the habit of drinking in the Cock Tavern opposite his house in Bow Street and had to keep all the windows open to convince his wife that there were no women with him. The loss of his pension and the death of his wife, who left him very little, resulted in Wycherley spending seven years in the Fleet debtors' prison. It was only when James II enquired about Wycherley's whereabouts and discovered his state that his debts were cancelled by royal command and his pension restored. He did marry again, this time in a fit of pique just eleven days before he died, 'to plague a damned nephew', his only heir.

W.B. YEATS
1865–1939

Yeats described his meeting with Maud Gonne as the beginning of 'the troubling of my life'. His unrequited, though not ultimately unconsummated, passion for her was to rule the next 30 years of his life. She became the great inspiration of his poetry, and in many ways his infatuation was the making of him as a poet. When Maud first met him, he was a struggling Irish poet in London and she a sophisticated English woman with a vague interest in Ireland. They shared an interest in Gaelic culture, extra-sensory perception and the occult, but not the same bed. Maud used Yeats to further her tenuous Irish links, something to which he willingly acceded in the hope of winning her love (he proposed to her more than 50 times), but she already had a lover, a Frenchman, Lucien Millevoye, by whom she had two daughters. The first child died young, and the second, Iseult Gonne, was introduced as an adopted cousin, though few people were fooled. She kept Yeats hanging on, summoning him to meet her wherever she was, either in Paris or Dublin, especially when she heard that he might be interested in another woman. The link was partially broken when Maud married 'Major' John McBride, an Irishman who had fought for the Boers against the British. This marriage was what she needed to bolster her credibility as an Irish patriot dedicated to the expulsion of the English from Ireland. The marriage only lasted two years, but it devastated Yeats, who, in spite of all the rejections still held out hope of marrying Maud. When McBride died, shot for his involvement in the Easter Rising of 1916, Yeats proposed to Maud yet again, and again was turned down. He then tried her daughter Iseult, by now a woman of 22. Yeats proposed — whether in desperation, in revenge, or in love we do not know — and he received the same dusty answer from the daughter as he had received time and again from the mother. At last he did marry, at 52, to Georgie Hyde Lees, another who shared his interest in the occult, and he went on producing great poetry to the end of his life, perhaps helped by his new wife and an experimental operation for rejuvenation, a vasectomy.

EPIGRAPH

'If, as Dr Johnson said, a man who is not married is
only half a man, so a man who is very much married
is only half a writer.'
CYRIL CONNOLLY *Enemies of Promise*

'Happy marriages, like happy nations, have no
history.'
MAURICE COLBOURN